Too Cute!

Baby Turtles

by Elizabeth Neuenfeldt

BELLWETHER MEDIA
MINNEAPOLIS, MN

Blastoff! Beginners are developed by literacy experts and educators to meet the needs of early readers. These engaging informational texts support young children as they begin reading about their world. Through simple language and high frequency words paired with crisp, colorful photos, Blastoff! Beginners launch young readers into the universe of independent reading.

Blastoff! Universe

Reading Level — Grade K

Grades 1-3

Grade 4

Sight Words in This Book 🔍

all	eat	it	some	they
are	find	look	soon	this
at	from	many	the	to
big	go	not	their	up
come	have	on	them	water
do	is	she	then	with

This edition first published in 2024 by Bellwether Media, Inc.

No part of this publication may be reproduced in whole or in part without written permission of the publisher. For information regarding permission, write to Bellwether Media, Inc., Attention: Permissions Department, 6012 Blue Circle Drive, Minnetonka, MN 55343.

Library of Congress Cataloging-in-Publication Data

Names: Neuenfeldt, Elizabeth, author.
Title: Baby turtles / by Elizabeth Neuenfeldt.
Description: Minneapolis, MN : Bellwether Media, 2024. | Series: Blastoff! Beginners: Too Cute! | Includes bibliographical references and index. | Audience: Ages 4-7 | Audience: Grades K-1
Identifiers: LCCN 2023039895 (print) | LCCN 2023039896 (ebook) | ISBN 9798886877755 (library binding) | ISBN 9798886878691 (ebook)
Subjects: LCSH: Turtles--Infancy--Juvenile literature.
Classification: LCC QL666.C5 N48 2024 (print) | LCC QL666.C5 (ebook) | DDC 597.92/139--dc23/eng/20230825
LC record available at https://lccn.loc.gov/2023039895
LC ebook record available at https://lccn.loc.gov/2023039896

Editor: Betsy Rathburn   Designer: Jeffrey Kollock

Printed in the United States of America, North Mankato, MN.

Table of Contents

A Baby Turtle!

Look at the
baby turtle.
Hello, hatchling!

On Their Own

Hatchlings come from eggs. Mom lays many eggs. Then she leaves.

mom

eggs

The hatchlings **hatch**.
They are tiny!
They have
small **shells**.

shell

Soon, they leave their **nest**. They do not go back.

nest

Some hatchlings
stay on land.
Some go
to water.

They find food.
They eat plants.
Some eat fish.

Hatchlings hide
from danger.
They stay safe!

hiding

All Grown Up

Hatchlings grow slowly. Their shells grow with them.

This hatchling
is very big.
It is all grown up!

Baby Turtle Facts

Turtle Life Stages

egg   hatchling   adult

A Day in the Life

go in
water   find food   hide

Glossary

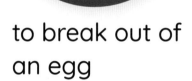

hatch

to break out of
an egg

nest

a home for
hatchlings

shells

hard coverings
on some animals

To Learn More

ON THE WEB

FACTSURFER

Factsurfer.com gives you a safe, fun way to find more information.

1. Go to www.factsurfer.com.

2. Enter "baby turtles" into the search box and click 🔍.

3. Select your book cover to see a list of related content.

Index